Remembering My Mom

A Guided Journal To Cherish Our Memories

Barbara L. Mason

Copyright © 2020 by
Barbara Mason
Written by Barbara Mason
All rights reserved. No part of this book may be
used or reproduced in any manner whatsoever
without the prior written permission of the author.

INTRODUCTION

My mom was my hero! And as I sat at her funeral and heard all the wonderful things her co-workers, friends and church members had to say about her, I realized that she was a living hero to many people and not just me.

My "hero" passed away in 2014 and my life changed forever that day in ways that words cannot express. Since that time, I have been on a mission to live a life of impact and be someone's hero daily just like my mom. When I do not know how or what to do, I remember all the examples she left me in our conversations and time together.

I decided to write this book because I want to help you remember your "mom-hero" in a very special way and give you a place to capture your most precious memories of the time spent with her. With each page, I have given you a memory prompt to capture your memories about your mom. Take one day a week to reflect on the moments you shared and allow them to bring you to a place of healing and strength but most of all, a deep heartfelt gratitude for being able to call her MOM.

With Love and Hope,

Barbara L. Mason

My proudest moment to be her daughter was when...

3 words that best describe my mom when I was growing up are...

_____
_____
_____
_____
_____
_____
_____
_____
_____
_____
_____
_____
_____
_____
_____
_____
_____
_____
_____
_____
_____
_____
_____
_____
_____

Once I became an adult, I would use these 3 words to describe my mom...

If I had 5 more minutes more with her, I would tell her....

The most special event I wish my mom could have seen was...

My mom's favorite color was....

She would wear it....

The word that best describes my mom's parenting style is....

_____

_____
_____
_____
_____
_____
_____
_____
_____
_____
_____
_____
_____
_____
_____
_____
_____
_____
_____
_____
_____
_____
_____
_____
_____
_____
_____

My friends thought my mom was....

_____

_____

_____

_____

_____

_____

_____

_____

_____

_____

_____

_____

_____

_____

_____

_____

_____

_____

_____

_____

_____

_____

_____

I love when my mom cooked...

I was so mad at my mom when ....

_____

_____

_____

_____

_____

_____

_____

_____

_____

_____

_____

_____

_____

_____

_____

_____

_____

_____

_____

_____

_____

_____

_____

_____

The personality trait I have most like my mom is...

_____

_____

_____

_____

_____

_____

_____

_____

_____

_____

_____

_____

_____

_____

_____

_____

_____

_____

_____

_____

_____

_____

_____

_____

I look like my mom by....

_____
_____
_____
_____
_____
_____
_____
_____
_____
_____
_____
_____
_____
_____
_____
_____
_____
_____
_____
_____
_____
_____
_____
_____

My mom's favorite saying when I was in trouble was...

_____ always reminds me of my mother...

The greatest life lesson my mother taught me is....

My funniest memory of my mother is...

_____
_____
_____
_____
_____
_____
_____
_____
_____
_____
_____
_____
_____
_____
_____
_____
_____
_____
_____
_____
_____
_____
_____

How do you want your mom to be remembered to your kids/others?

_____
_____
_____
_____
_____
_____
_____
_____
_____
_____
_____
_____
_____
_____
_____
_____
_____
_____
_____
_____
_____
_____
_____
_____
_____

I thought my mom would kill me when I...

My mom's best advice to me was...

One thing I've done since she passed away that she would be proud of is....

My mom was most surprised when I....

_____
_____
_____
_____
_____
_____
_____
_____
_____
_____
_____
_____
_____
_____
_____
_____
_____
_____
_____
_____
_____
_____
_____
_____
_____

My mom's favorite things were...

The worst thing my mom cooked was....

The best meal my mom ever cooked was....

_____

_____

_____

_____

_____

_____

_____

_____

_____

_____

_____

_____

_____

_____

_____

_____

_____

_____

_____

_____

_____

_____

_____

_____

_____

Inside jokes I had with my mom....

My mom always made me wear...

My mom always hated when I....

I saw my mom cry when....

The best holiday I shared with my mom is...

My mom always wanted to do _____ on her birthday...

_____

_____
_____
_____
_____
_____
_____
_____
_____
_____
_____
_____
_____
_____
_____
_____
_____
_____
_____
_____
_____
_____
_____

My mom always said I did this when I was a baby...

When I was upset, my mom would....

The thing I used to always do with my mom was....

One thing I kept from my mom was...

I wish I could have told my mom...

The one regret I have regarding my mom is....

My mom's favorite game was...

_____
_____
_____
_____
_____
_____
_____
_____
_____
_____
_____
_____
_____
_____
_____
_____
_____
_____
_____
_____
_____
_____
_____
_____
_____

My mom's favorite restaurant was..

The one thing that would make my mom laugh was...

The one thing that my mom would do to make me laugh was....

_____

_____

_____

_____

_____

_____

_____

_____

_____

_____

_____

_____

_____

_____

_____

_____

_____

_____

_____

_____

_____

_____

_____

_____

My mom was afraid of...

My mom and I's best trip together was...

My mom's favorite thing to wear was...

My mom was disappointed when I...

Best character trait I got from my mom is....

_____
_____
_____
_____
_____
_____
_____
_____
_____
_____
_____
_____
_____
_____
_____
_____
_____
_____
_____
_____
_____
_____
_____
_____
_____
_____
_____

One of the biggest sacrifices my mom made for our family was...

The friend that my mom disliked the most was....

The guy my mom wanted me to marry is...

My mom would always tell me to _____ when I left the house.

_____

_____

_____

_____

_____

_____

_____

_____

_____

_____

_____

_____

_____

_____

_____

_____

_____

_____

_____

_____

_____

_____

_____

_____

_____

_____

Her favorite thing to do on the weekend was...

I have kept _____ to remind me of her

Everytime I see/smell/hear _____, I think of my mom

_____
_____
_____
_____
_____
_____
_____
_____
_____
_____
_____
_____
_____
_____
_____
_____
_____
_____
_____
_____
_____
_____
_____
_____

After my mom passed away, it took me the longest to...

I will never forget when my mom said...

My mom and I would talk on the phone about ......

The last thing my mom and I did together was....

My mom's favorite room in the house was..

58.   I sound just like my mom when I say '_____"...

_____
_____
_____
_____
_____
_____
_____
_____
_____
_____
_____
_____
_____
_____
_____
_____
_____
_____
_____
_____
_____
_____
_____
_____
_____

One of my mom's rules I hated the most was...

_____
_____
_____
_____
_____
_____
_____
_____
_____
_____
_____
_____
_____
_____
_____
_____
_____
_____
_____
_____
_____
_____
_____
_____
_____

The best thing I could do to honor my mom's legacy is....

Made in the USA
Las Vegas, NV
30 July 2023

75418303R00037